# PRAGUE

METRO BOOKS
New York

An Imprint of Sterling Publishing Co., Inc.
1166 Avenue of the Americas
New York, NY 10036

ISBN 978-1-4351-6810-7

For information about custom editions, special sales, and premium
and corporate purchases, please contact Sterling Special Sales
at 800-805-5489 or specialsales@sterlingpublishing.com.

Manufactured in China

2 4 6 8 10 9 7 5 3 1

www.sterlingpublishing.com

© Texts: Josef Černá
Translator: Natalie Danford
Designer: Matteo Gaule

Josef Černá

# PRAGUE

METRO BOOKS
NEW YORK

# CONTENTS

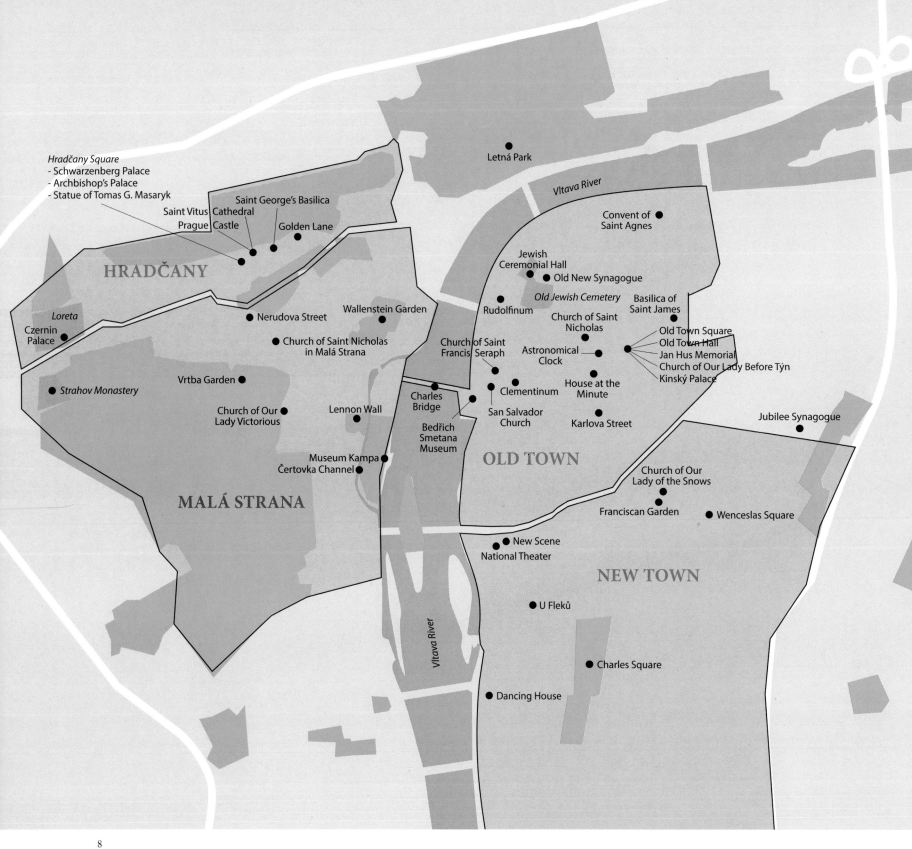

Hradčany Square
- Schwarzenberg Palace
- Archbishop's Palace
- Statue of Tomas G. Masaryk

Saint George's Basilica

Saint Vitus Cathedral

Prague Castle

Golden Lane

HRADČANY

Loreta

Czernin Palace

Nerudova Street

Wallenstein Garden

Church of Saint Nicholas in Malá Strana

Vrtba Garden

Strahov Monastery

Church of Our Lady Victorious

Lennon Wall

Charles Bridge

Bedřich Smetana Museum

Museum Kampa

Čertovka Channel

MALÁ STRANA

Letná Park

Vltava River

Convent of Saint Agnes

Jewish Ceremonial Hall

Old New Synagogue

Old Jewish Cemetery

Rudolfinum

Basilica of Saint James

Church of Saint Nicholas

Church of Saint Francis Seraph

Astronomical Clock

Old Town Square
Old Town Hall
Jan Hus Memorial
Church of Our Lady Before Týn
Kinský Palace

Clementinum

San Salvador Church

House at the Minute

Karlova Street

OLD TOWN

Jubilee Synagogue

Church of Our Lady of the Snows

Franciscan Garden

Wenceslas Square

New Scene

National Theater

NEW TOWN

U Fleků

Vltava River

Charles Square

Dancing House

# INTRODUCTION

Prague is magical. It's a shame that that has become a bit of a tourist cliché, because Prague truly is a place of enchantment. This city built on the shores of the Vltava River is unique. It boasts a mystical mix of Gothic and baroque styles, and it is a seemingly unending collection of towers and domes, squares, streams, and hills. It is graced with sparkling touches and ancient inscriptions, and a population of statues that overlook it all. What makes Prague exceptional—truly magical—is that it is not a dusty museum exhibit. Despite its dense and complex history, it is a place that lives and moves just as surely as the hands, spheres, and figures of the famous astronomical clock in Old Town do. Prague is a relatively small city, yet it has more than its share of incomparable sights, from the grand to the minuscule. There are sweeping views into the far distance, with the kind of broad horizons and intense golden light that call to mind the music of Bedřich Smetana, the city's ever-present soundtrack. But there are also numerous narrow alleys, small streets and squares, and other secluded spots that feel like secret discoveries. It is an urban place with a bustling center and a capital city's dense architecture, but it also offers nature in the center of the city in the form of its large river, but also via gardens, parks, and wooded hilly areas such as Petřín.

And Prague has its roots in magic. On Vyšehrad, a rocky cliff that overlooks a curve in the Vltava River, just before the year 1000, when this area was still completely untamed, the princess Libuše—who with her husband, Přemysl, would go on to found the first royal dynasty of Bohemia—is said to have spoken these prophetic words: "I see a great city whose glory will touch the stars!" The story continues that she then ordered a carpenter to build a symbolic threshold (a *praha*): a doorway that opened into thin air, as the capital still existed only in her imagination. Over the centuries, the city developed on both sides of the river, not as a single city, but as two separate areas. Until the late eighteenth century, the various neighborhoods that today comprise Prague were all individual cities, each with its own town hall, walls, and character. The right bank, which is relatively flat, saw the growth of Old Town (Staré Město, with its large Jewish quarter) and New Town (Nové Město), where many markets were installed because there

was so much open space. The other side of the river is a green hilly slope, and its development reflects that: this is where you will find densely populated Malá Strana (literally "the little part") on the hillside and above it at the top of the hill the castle neighborhood. This area developed over centuries, but its starring attraction is undoubtedly that iconic castle, the locus of so much European history. The transfer of the court in about 1140 signaled the beginning of the abandonment of the original Vyšehrad castle and jump-started the city's development. The reign of Charles IV, King of Bohemia (1355-1478) was a critical moment in the history of Prague. It was largely at this time that Prague became one of the most beautiful Gothic cities in the world. Charles designed a road to cross the city and lead over the Charles Bridge to the castle. The influence of Charles IV on the city's architecture and its layout is still visible today. During that time, when the city was flourishing, a papal nuncio wrote to the pope, "I don't know whether cities such as Rome, Venice, Florence and others around the world can ever compete in beauty with this pearl in the heart of Europe." Prague became part of the Habsburg empire and then its capital (taking that role from Vienna) under Emperor Rudolf II, an eccentric figure (to say the least) who shaped Prague further with his longstanding interest in alchemy, the occult, collecting exotic objects, and his relationship with the local Jewish community and interest in the Kabbalah. The legend of the Golem is said to have developed during his reign. The Thirty Years' War broke out after the Defenestration of Prague, which involved imperial regents. The war left devastation in its wake; the Swedish invasion was particularly harsh. Prague was later rebuilt and given a new baroque look reflected in its churches and statues. That style would remain in place throughout successive historical and architectural periods. Particularly notable are the local Art Nouveau style that flourished during the era of Franz Kafka and the later cubist architectural style. Prague was occupied by Nazis but remained largely unscathed by World War II (when again it was ascribed magical properties said to have protected it), and then for the fifty years that Czechoslovakia was a Soviet satellite, Prague served as its capital. When the country was divided into the Czech Republic and Slovakia in 1989, Prague was greatly energized. Many buildings were restored to their previous splendor, and the city's museums developed into some of the world's finest.

PP. 4-5: THE ROOFTOPS, SPIRES, AND STEEPLES OF PRAGUE REPRESENT A RANGE OF ERAS AND STYLES. GOLD GLINTS EVERYWHERE IN OLD TOWN.

P. 6: THE BEDŘICH SMETANA MUSEUM IS LOCATED IN A NEORENAISSANCE BUILDING THAT WAS ONCE HOME TO A WATER COMPANY AND SITS ALONG A RIVERBANK PROMENADE.

P. 7: THE WINDING VLTAVA RIVER SEEN FROM THE STRAHOV MONASTERY GARDENS; THE CHARLES BRIDGE IS AT THE RIGHT. IN THE CENTER, NEAR THE MÁNES BRIDGE, IS THE LARGE RUDOLFINUM BUILDING. THE HILL ON THE LEFT IS LETNÁ.

P. 9: THE CHARLES BRIDGE, DESIGNED IN THE MID-1300S, WAS BUILT TO BE STURDY ENOUGH TO WITHSTAND THE RUSHING RIVER.

P. 10: THE CASTLE'S ADMINISTRATIVE WINGS AND ITS GOTHIC CATHEDRAL DOMINATE THE MALÁ STRANA AREA. TO THE FAR LEFT IS THE BLACK TOWER, ONE OF ONLY THREE ENTRANCES TO THE CASTLE.

OPPOSITE: CELETNÁ CAN BE SEEN CLEARLY FROM THE TOP OF POWDER TOWER. THIS MAIN STREET IS NOW A WIDE PEDESTRIAN WALKWAY THROUGH OLD TOWN. THE GOTHIC CHURCH OF OUR LADY BEFORE TÝN (LEFT) AND THE ANCIENT BASILICA OF SAINT JAMES (RIGHT), WHICH WAS REBUILT IN THE LATE SEVENTEENTH CENTURY, ARE BOTH PRAGUE LANDMARKS.

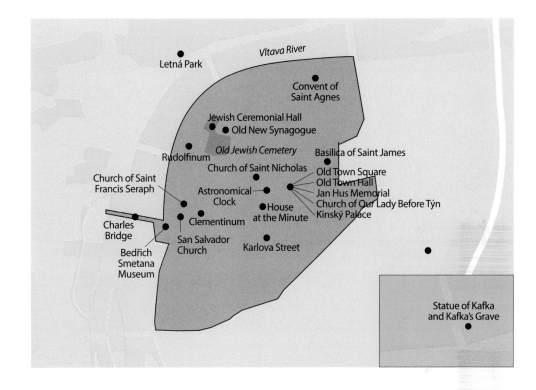

The largest and most significant area in the historic center of Prague formed during the Middle Ages around an enormous square with the Church of Our Lady Before Týn on one side and the Old Town Hall on the other, each topped with towers and steeples. Historic houses with pediments on the sides of the square lend the scene a fairytale quality that is enhanced further by the stone ghosts emerging from the Jan Hus Memorial and the cheery baroque domes on the Church of Saint Nicholas. The Old Town, a maze of shadowed doorways and dreamy little squares, runs along the length of the Royal Route until it reaches the Charles Bridge. This is the two-and-a-half-mile (four-kilometer) route that Charles IV walked between the city's two major castles. Over the centuries, buildings have been constructed along this path. They include aristocratic palaces, convents, and cultural touchstones. As time passed, the Gothic style gave way to a more Italian-influenced version, and then later to the exuberance of the baroque and rococo. The notes of Mozart's Don Giovanni seem to play everywhere here, and the opera is closely connected to the city. Elegant Parížská Street leads from Old Town Square to Josefov, once the city's Jewish ghetto. The large number of synagogues here is a testament to the size and importance of the city's Jewish population at one time, and the Old Jewish Cemetery is yet another somber and touching reminder of Prague's past.

Pp. 16-17: The eighteenth-century Church of Saint Nicholas sits on the main square in Old Town. Tree-lined Parížská Street is an elegant boulevard that leads into the Jewish quarter. On the other side of the bridge in the distance the Prague Metronome, an art installation that dates to 1991, can be glimpsed in the background.

Opposite: One of the busiest parts of Prague is the square that gives access to the Charles Bridge, squeezed between the Jesuit San Salvador Church and the domes of the Church of Saint Francis Seraph. The Artbanka Museum of Young Art has been located in the eighteenth-century Colloredo Palace, right, since 2011.

Pp. 20-21: Pastel-colored houses with porticos surround Old Town Square.

19

◄ ## OLD TOWN SQUARE ►►
### *Staroměstské náměstí*

The spiky steeples of the Church of Our Lady Before Týn tower over lively Old Town Square, the site of coronations and other public ceremonies, open-air markets, and even hangings. This is the center of Prague's history and identity, for better and for worse. Each building tells a story, but the most evocative tale is told by the combination of different architectural styles, the Gothic and baroque, stones and plaster, steeples and statues. From an aerial viewpoint, you can see the space between Old Town Hall and the Church of Saint Nicholas: this was created when a wing of the Old Town Hall was destroyed during Nazi occupation, the only significant damage to a major building in Prague during World War II.

## JAN HUS MEMORIAL
*Památník Mistra Jana Husa*

The Jan Hus Memorial was built beginning in 1900 based on a design by Jan Šaloun. The monument stands on the spot where Jan Hus was burned at the stake for heresy in 1415. Hus was the rector of the University of Prague and a religious and political reformer. The large monument is an outstanding example of the Secese style, Bohemia's own Art Nouveau.

# OLD TOWN HALL

*Staroměstská radnice*

Old Town Hall is located in Old Town on a lovely square, and it is one of Prague's landmark buildings. It is actually a complex comprising a group of varied buildings that over the years clustered around the dark stone base of the fourteenth-century clock tower with its famed astronomical dial. Among these buildings is a Renaissance-style structure that features a characteristic three-part window with the phrase "Praga caput regni" written above it.

# ASTRONOMICAL CLOCK
## *Staroměstský Orloj*

For more than six hundred years, visitors to Old Town have flocked to see the astronomical clock, or *orloj*, at Old Town Hall. The original mechanism dates to 1410, and it was considered a true technical marvel in its time. The clock was rebuilt in the fifteenth and sixteenth centuries and was recently restored. The top two quadrants of the clock show the time, the position of the sun and moon, and the zodiac. Various figures, some of which appear in two windows, perform ritual moves on the hour.

# HOUSE AT THE MINUTE
## *Dům U Minuty*

▶

The birthplace of Prague literary lion Franz Kafka is found in the Jewish quarter, but from 1889 to 1896 the Kafka family lived in this centrally located house near Old Town Hall in Old Town, known as the House at the Minute (as in small). The building's facade is decorated with intricate Renaissance-style sgraffito that dates to the era of Rudolf II. The allegorical scenes combine a mix of Bible stories and secular legends.

# ◀ CHURCH OF OUR LADY BEFORE TÝN ▶
## *Kostel Matky Boží před Týnem*

Týn is a large courtyard in Prague's Old Town once used as a marketplace and customs office and flanked by the Church of Our Lady Before Týn and the Basilica of Saint James. The former church resembles a mother hen surrounded by her chicks, as it is encircled entirely by houses and other buildings. Yet this excellent example of the fourteenth-century Gothic style rises above them and commands attention with its towers and steeples. The interior (entered by way of a narrow alley) is no less impressive and strikes a somber tone in striking contrast to the lively air of the square outside.

OPPOSITE: THE KINSKÝ PALACE (LEFT OF THE CHURCH FAÇADE) IS DE-
CORATED WITH EYE-CATCHING STUCCOES IN VARIOUS COLORS TYPICAL
OF THE ROCOCO ARCHITECTURE FAVORED BY THE LOCAL ARISTOCRACY
IN THE MID-1700S. TODAY THE BUILDING HOUSES THE CONTEMPORARY
ART WING OF THE PRAGUE NATIONAL GALLERY.

NÁRODNÍ GALERIE

◀

# KINSKÝ PALACE
### *Palác Kinských*

Kinský Palace is one of Prague's rococo gems. It sits on a corner of Old Town Square near the Church of Our Lady Before Týn. Now part of the Prague National Gallery complex, it is the backdrop for exhibitions of contemporary art and photography.

# CHURCH OF SAINT NICHOLAS
## *Kostel sv. Mikuláše*

Prague's various districts were originally autonomous, each its own small city, which explains why modern Prague often has multiple churches devoted to the same saint. Saint Nicholas has lent his name to two different eighteenth-century churches, one in Old Town and the other in Malá Strana. The Church of Saint Nicholas on Old Town Square was designed by Klian Dietzenhofer and is a witty play of curved lines and domes.

## CHARLES BRIDGE
### *Karlův most*

Charles Bridge is one of the highlights of a visit to Prague. King Charles IV designed the bridge in the mid-1300s. It

crosses the Vltava as part of the route between the Vyšehrad and Hradčany castles and connects Old Town to Malá Strana. There is also a staircase off the bridge onto Kampa Island. Just under 1,700 feet (a little over 500 meters) long, it is supported by sixteen arches with sharply geometric bases

designed to withstand rising water levels. Gothic gates stand
guard at each end, and the towers were once customs offices.
The bridge was a marvel of engineering for its time.

OPPOSITE, ABOVE, AND FOLLOWING: THE BRIDGE IS LINED ON BOTH SIDES
BY A SERIES OF INVENTIVE BAROQUE STATUES, MOST OF WHICH DATE TO THE
EARLY 1700S. IN THE NINETEENTH-CENTURY, A STATUE OF THE KING HIMSELF
WAS ERECTED IN A SMALL GARDEN NEAR THE ENTRANCE ON THE OLD TOWN
SIDE OF THE BRIDGE.

51

## CHURCH OF SAINT FRANCIS SERAPH
### *Kostel sv. Františka Serafinského*

The seventeenth-century Church of Saint Francis Seraph stands in the square at one end of the Charles Bridge. Despite its small footprint, the church feels large because of its dome—decorated with elaborate frescoes—and its Greek-cross plan.

## SAN SALVADOR CHURCH
### *Kostel Nejsvetejšího Salvátora*

The late-Renaissance façade of San Salvador Church, graced with a portico and a rich array of statues, was designed by Italian architects. The Jesuit church is part of the Clementinum complex. Classical music concerts take advantage of both the pretty setting and the excellent acoustics.

## KARLOVA STREET
### *Karlova*

Karlova Street is the portion of the Royal Route that runs from Old Town Square to the Charles Bridge and alongside the large Clementinum. It was named for Charles IV. The winding street remains unchanged since the Middle Ages, as do many of the decorations on its buildings, though it is now lined with modern stores and is one of the busiest areas of Prague.

◄

## RUDOLFINUM
### *Galerie Rudolfinum*

The Rudolfinum, a theater-auditorium and cultural center built circa 1880, looms over Jan Palach Square in Old Town. (Palach was a student who immolated himself in protest on January 16, 1969.) The Czech Philharmonic Orchestra performs here.

## BEDŘICH SMETANA MUSEUM
### *Muzeum Bedřicha Smetany*

The Bedřich Smetana Museum in Prague enjoys a splendid location on the banks of the river, making it beloved not only for its contents, but as a subject for photography. Czech composer Smetana wrote a symphonic poem in 1874 that is an ode to the Vltava River (and part of a composition titled "My Country"). By that time the composer had become completely deaf, so he was never able to hear his own masterpiece.

## CLEMENTINUM
### *Klementinum*

Jesuits broke ground to begin building the Clementinum complex in the mid-1600s. Today it includes a large number of buildings connected by ten different courtyards. Staircases, chapels, museum collections, libraries, and areas for science and research join together in a true labyrinth of knowledge.

## JUBILEE SYNAGOGUE
### *Jeruzalémská synagoga (Jubilejní)*

The Jubilee Synagogue was named in honor of the five hundredth anniversary of the reign of Emperor Franz Joseph I. It was originally known as the Jerusalem Synagogue. Built from 1905 to 1906 in an unusual Art Nouveau style, the synagogue has 850 seats, making it the largest Jewish house of worship in Prague. The city once had a very large Jewish population both in the former Jewish ghetto and outside of it. The Jubilee Synagogue sits on the outskirts of Old Town.

## JEWISH QUARTER
### *Josefov*

In the late nineteenth century, tree-lined Pařížská Street was created to run from Old Town Square to the banks of the Vltava. This had the effect of opening up Josefov, Prague's traditional Jewish neighborhood and one-time ghetto, and Jewish residents of Prague began to spread out and live in other parts of the city. Josefov is still home to many sites that recall earlier Jewish life in Prague, including a number of large synagogues, a museum dedicated to Jewish culture, and the Old Jewish Cemetery.

## OLD NEW SYNAGOGUE
*Staronová synagoga*

The Old New Synagogue of Prague is the oldest active synagogue in Europe. Built in the thirteenth century, the original building exhibited a Romanesque-Gothic style, but over the centuries it has been modified. Though the origin of its unusual name is uncertain, the building itself is extraordinary. This synagogue, another four synagogues, and the Jewish Ceremonial Hall used for funeral services are all in the care of the Jewish Museum in Prague, as is the Jewish cemetery.

## JEWISH CEREMONIAL HALL
*Obřadní síň*

The neo-medieval Jewish Ceremonial Hall, built in 1911, is part of the Jewish Museum in Prague, along with several synagogues and the Old Jewish Cemetery. The museum's collections are distributed among these buildings, with textiles and silver items in Maisel Synagogue, items from everyday life in Klausen Synagogue, and drawings by children imprisoned in the Theresienstadt concentration camp in Pinkas Synagogue.

# OLD JEWISH CEMETERY
## *Starý Židovský Hřbitov*

This small, dense cemetery contains more than 12,000 graves. It was in use from the fifteenth to the eighteenth centuries. Old tombstones, many of them sloping and worn away by time, stand in close proximity under the trees. Judah Loew, a rabbi who was said to advise Rudolf II on esoteric matters, is buried in a corner.

## ◄ STATUE OF KAFKA AND KAFKA'S GRAVE ►
### *Pomník Kafky - Hrob Kafky*

In 2004 a bronze statue honoring Franz Kafka was installed near the Spanish Synagogue. The work, by sculptor Jaroslav Róna, depicts a man seated on the shoulders of a headless giant, an image straight out of Kafka's famously surreal imagination. Kafka isn't buried in the nearby Jewish cemetery, however; instead his grave can be found in Strašnice. The writer's many fans often leave messages for him, or place pebbles on his headstone as a sign of respect.

## CONVENT OF SAINT AGNES
### *Klášter sv. Anežky České*

This impressive thirteenth-century complex sits right on the banks of the Vltava (and has been damaged by rising waters many times). The Medieval collection of the Prague National Gallery, which contains many fourteenth-century paintings from the Bohemian school, is exhibited here.

## BASILICA OF SAINT JAMES ▶
### *Kostel sv. Jakuba Staršího*

A fire that devastated Prague's Old Town in 1689 wrought heavy damage to the Basilica of Saint James. The church was rebuilt immediately, though, and it is decorated with ornate baroque stuccos.

## LETNÁ PARK
### *Letenské sady*

This park is across the river from Old Town, but it sits on a hill that provides a verdant backdrop to many views of the city center. A large monument to Joseph Stalin once stood on the platform at the crest of the hill, but in 1991 it was removed and a gigantic metronome almost eighty feet (twenty-five meters) tall by Vratislav Novák was installed to "keep time" for the newly energized city.

The gardens in the park offer incredible views of the Vltava. The ornate Hanavský Pavilion, a neo-baroque building that dates to 1891, is now a restaurant.

◀

# VLTAVA RIVER
## *Vltava*

The Vltava River doesn't simply run through Prague—it has shaped Prague with a firm hand. Indeed, this river runs through all of the Czech Republic for 267 miles (430 kilometers) and then merges with the Elbe. The river has overflowed its banks, flooding Prague and causing great damage, many times, most recently in 2002 and 2013.

# New Town

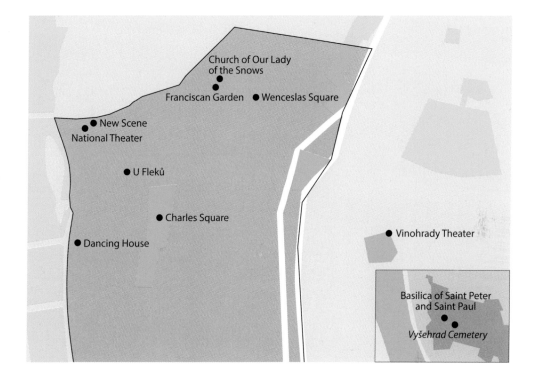

Until the mid-fourteenth century, Prague's historic center was blocked off to the south by a ditch crossed by a small bridge. King Charles IV decided to organize the entire area at the foot of the Vyšehrad castle hill and create a "New Town" that would offer room for the overflow from densely populated Old Town and would also contain a series of large marketplace squares for the sale of horses, cows, and hay. What was "new" about this area of the city was the kind of urban-planning involved, which was highly innovative for the 1300s. The layout adopted still exists, though many of the actual buildings date to the nineteenth and twentieth centuries. The heart of New Town is Wenceslas Square, home to the Czech National Museum. An equestrian statue of Saint Wenceslas and a flowerbed commemorating Jan Palach, the student who immolated himself to protest the Soviet repression of the Prague Spring in 1968, are featured. Wide boulevards lined with pubs cross New Town and lead to the shores of the river and national theater. The shady Franciscan Garden is accessed via covered passageways tucked behind the enormous Gothic Church of Our Lady of the Snows, which was never completed.

## CHARLES SQUARE
*Karlovo náměstí*

Charles Square was part of the thoughtfully conceived late Medieval layout of New Town, and it was originally intended to be used as a market for livestock. It is the largest square in Prague. Eventually, the square was turned into a public park. Every other Sunday a small antiques market is held in the square, and students from the nearby university frequently take their breaks here. On one side of the square there is a large baroque Jesuit school building, and the tall tower of New Town Hall, dating to the fifteenth and sixteenth centuries, overlooks the surrounding area.

## WENCESLAS SQUARE
### *Václavské náměstí*  ▶ ▶▶

This square named for the patron saint slopes slightly through Old Town. This is a Prague landmark and the center of political life in Prague. Protests held here have set in motion events that rocked this city and the entire country. The buildings around the square date to the late nineteenth and early twentieth centuries, offering a mix of historicist and Art Nouveau styles. The equestrian statue of Saint Wenceslas stands at the top of the incline along with four other statues of saints with ties to Bohemia; these were added beginning in 1888.

◀

# NATIONAL THEATER
## *Národní Divadlo*

The National Theater (a neorenaissance building designed by Josef Zítek and completed in 1881) figures strongly in the cultural identity of Prague. This large building sits on the banks of the Vltava near the 1901 Legion Bridge. Performances include classical music concerts and opera.

## NEW SCENE ▶
### *Nová Scéna*

This modern 1983 building is part of the adjacent National Theater and is made of 4,000 blown glass blocks. The Lanterna Magica theater company performs music and dance here.

## VINOHRADY THEATER ▶
### *Divadlo na Vinohradech*

When New Town and Wenceslas Square expanded in the nineteenth century, an area planted with vineyards was transformed into an urban setting, but it kept the name Vinohrady, or vineyard. The center of this city-within-a-city is Peace Square, which is surrounded by Art Nouveau-style buildings, including this beautiful theater from the early twentieth century.

## ◄ CHURCH OF OUR LADY OF THE SNOWS
### *Kostel Panny Marie Sněžné*

The Gothic Church of Our Lady of the Snows was designed to be one of the largest churches in Prague, but only a portion of it, the choir area—now surrounded by a simple exterior—was constructed.

## FRANCISCAN GARDEN ►
### *Františkánská zahrada*

In 1603, Franciscan monks took possession of the Church of Our Lady of the Snows. A lovely garden planted with fruit trees was created on the grounds of the cemetery, creating a tranquil spot in New Town that offers a good view of the church's fourteenth-century choir area.

## U FLEKŮ
*U Fleků*

In New Town, a wide variety of restaurants and pubs (*pivnice*) serve traditional and tasty Bohemian food. Prague's most famous pub is U Fleků, which serves dark, smooth beer that has been made according to the same recipe since 1499.

## DANCING HOUSE
*Tančící dům*

Prague has many beautiful historic buildings, but it is also fertile ground for innovative architecture. Among the interesting modern buildings in the city is Frank Gehry's "Dancing House," designed for an insurance company. It sits on the Vltava and adds a refreshing contemporary note to the architecture in the area.

Opposite: The "Dancing House" consists of two parts that are completely different from each other, but seem to be joined in an embrace, as if they were dancing. The building is sometimes called "Fred and Ginger" in a reference to Fred Astaire and Ginger Rogers. The glass tower is slim and elegant; the stone portion that balances on a single pillar has a more solid look.

## ◀ BASILICA OF SAINT PETER AND SAINT PAUL ▶
### *Sv. Petr a Pavel na Vyšehradě*

Architect Josef Mocker was the mastermind behind this nineteenth-century neogothic revival church. The church was built in 1885 on the remains of a previous building. Signature features include two twin steeples and intricate ornamental details—such as the mosaic entryway—that marked a move away from Medieval style and toward a more heightened symbolism.

Above and opposite: Elaborate detail, including a stunning mosaic entryway, makes the Basilica of Saint Peter and Saint Paul unique.

## VYŠEHRAD CEMETERY
*Vyšehradský hřbitov*

The old parish cemetery connected to the Basilica of Saint Peter and Saint Paul includes the Slavín, a pantheon where famous local figures were laid to rest. The cemetery was active in the nineteenth and twentieth century. Architects, painters, sculptors, and musicians are buried here.

101

# MALÁ STRANA

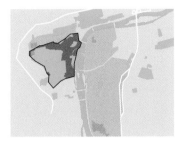

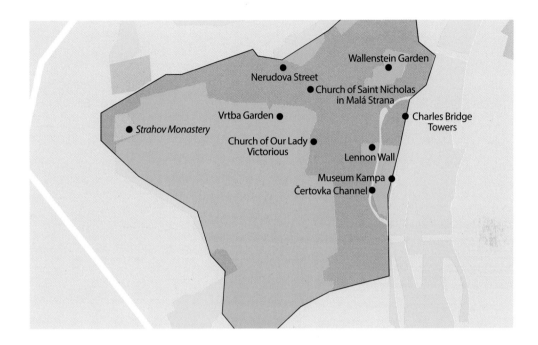

Wallenstein Garden

Nerudova Street

Church of Saint Nicholas
in Malá Strana

Vrtba Garden

Charles Bridge
Towers

Strahov Monastery

Church of Our Lady
Victorious

Lennon Wall

Museum Kampa

Čertovka Channel

The Charles Bridge is the most famous symbol of Prague. It connects neighborhoods that had historically been fiercely proud of their autonomy. It is a fantastic stone structure that both stands out from and blends with the waters rushing below it. And it leads to the most beloved neighborhood in Prague: Malá Strana, the "little part" of the city on the left bank of the Vltava. This neighborhood overflows with gardens, palaces, and churches, packed tightly against each other. It is an unending array of staircases, balconies, domes, and steeples, and many of its streets drop at breathtaking angles. It is at the same time the area most closely identified with Prague and a place that is quite international and cosmopolitan in its architecture and general feel. Nerudova Street and Vlašská ("Italian Street") lead to the Strahov Monastery of the Premonstratensians and are the city's prettiest streets. Starting from the busy square where the large Church of Saint Michael the Archangel is located, you can walk uphill amid sumptuous residences that belonged to aristocratic families at one time. Gradually the architecture becomes more rustic: there are stone walls here and there, and votive niches, as well as open spaces. Here, just minutes from the Prague Castle, the city feels instead like rural countryside, dotted with vineyards and woods. The monastery with its frescoed library and cultural treasures is a quiet spot suitable for sinking deep into thought, or possibly prayer and contemplation.

## NERUDOVA STREET
*Nerudova*

Malá Strana stretches along the steep bank of the river and up to the castle. This area is densely built, and at a glance there seem to be few buildings that date to later than the eighteenth century. Elegant baroque details lend the neighborhood its special character.

# CHURCH OF SAINT NICHOLAS IN MALÁ STRANA

*Kostel sv. Mikuláše na Malé Straně*

The buildings in Malá Strana seem to stand almost on top of one another, as they are so tightly constructed on the neighborhood's steep hills. The Church of Saint Nicholas on the area's main square is a noticeable exception. Designed in 1703 by Cristoph Dietzenhofer, this large late baroque church was completed more than half a century later. It boasts lavish decoration, including a tall dome and a charming bell tower, both clad in copper.

ABOVE AND OPPOSITE: THE LOVELY CHURCH OF SAINT NICHOLAS IS
JOYFUL AND WELCOMING. THE LARGE FRESCOES IN THE INTERIOR EMPLOY
SOPHISTICATED PERSPECTIVE AND COMBINE WITH THE LIGHT THAT SHINES IN
THROUGH LARGE WINDOWS, STUCCOS, AND OTHER FURNISHINGS TO CREATE A
SENSE OF PERPETUAL MOTION.

111

## CHURCH OF OUR LADY VICTORIOUS
### *Kostel Panny Marie Vítězné*

This Lutheran church became a Catholic place of worship after the Thirty Years' War. The compact baroque building sits amid the green gardens of the seminary. It is known best for the Infant Jesus of Prague, a small sixteenth-century wax statue.

◄ ## CHARLES BRIDGE TOWERS
### *Věže - Karlův most*

On the Malá Strana side of the Charles Bridge there is a Gothic arch and two towers: the smaller tower was part of fortifications that date to the twelfth century, while the taller Gothic tower dates to the 1400s. Visitors can enjoy sweeping views of Prague's historic center from its balcony.

ABOVE: THE GOTHIC ARCHES AT THE ENDS OF THE BRIDGE ARE
DECORATED WITH STATUES AND COATS OF ARMS LINKED TO BOHEMIA.
OPPOSITE: THE PILLARS OF THE CHARLES BRIDGE, AT EYE LEVEL
WITH THE WATER, VIEWED FROM KAMPA ISLAND. IN THE FOURTEENTH
CENTURY THE BRIDGE WAS CONSTRUCTED ON TOP OF AN EXISTING
STONE STRUCTURE THAT DATED TO THE TWELFTH CENTURY.

## ČERTOVKA CHANNEL
### *Čertovka*

The waters of the Vltava rise and fall, of course, and the resulting changes in water levels have had impact on the riverbanks and the surrounding area. A narrow waterway between Kampa Island and the Malá Strana riverbank has become known as the Čertovka Channel, literally "devil's channel." Picturesque water mills have been built along the channel.

◄

# MUSEUM KAMPA
## *Museum Kampa*

Quiet, shady Kampa Island is very different from Malá Strana, with its aristocratic air. A modern art museum with an excellent collection of twentieth-century painting and sculpture is housed in a nineteenth-century mill on the island.

# LENNON WALL
## *Lennonova zeď*

The Order of Malta owns an area in Malá Strana near the river that is home to several major historical buildings. The focus of the area is Grand Priory Square. This is also the location of the Lennon Wall, so named for its graffiti depictions of former Beatle John Lennon. In the 1980s, the Soviet-backed government banned Lennon's music; the graffiti on this wall—which also includes lyrics to some of his songs—was a daring sign of rebellion.

# VRTBA GARDEN
## *Vrtbovská zahrada*

These gorgeous baroque gardens were restored beginning in 1990 and progressively reopened to the public. They are laid out around elegant buildings on the slopes of the hills in this part of the city. Such manicured gardens and plantings render a clear idea of the life of nobility in Prague in earlier days. The garden sits on five levels and includes flowerbeds, rare plants, fruit trees, and decorative elements.

## WALLENSTEIN GARDEN
### *Valdštejnská zahrada*

Even in Malá Strana, where beautiful baroque buildings abound, Wallenstein Palace—which originally belonged to Duke Albrecht von Wallenstein, commander-in-chief of the imperial army during the Thirty Years' War—stands out. The palace was designed by Italian architects and is known best for its outstanding garden, which backs up against the building that once served as a stable.

ABOVE AND OPPOSITE: THE GARDEN PATHS ARE DECORATED WITH
COPIES OF BRONZE STATUES BY DUTCH ARTIST ADRIAEN DE VRIES.
THE ORIGINALS WERE BROUGHT TO STOCKHOLM BY THE SWEDISH
ARMY AFTER IT SACKED PRAGUE IN 1648.

## STRAHOV MONASTERY
### *Strahovský klášter*

▶

This Premonstratensian monastery atop a hill in Strahov was built in the twelfth century, but completely rebuilt in the seventeenth and eighteenth centuries, when it was transformed into one of the leading European baroque culture centers.

ABOVE AND OPPOSITE: THE STRAHOV MONASTERY STANDS AS A CITADEL OF FAITH AND KNOWLEDGE. IT HOUSES TWO OUTSTANDING LIBRARIES: THE LATE BAROQUE PHILOSOPHICAL HALL, DECORATED WITH STUCCOS, AND THE LATE-EIGHTEENTH-CENTURY THEOLOGICAL HALL, WITH ITS GILDED BOOKSHELVES AND WONDERFUL ROCOCO FRESCOES BY FRANZ ANTON MAULPERTSCH.

# HRADČANY

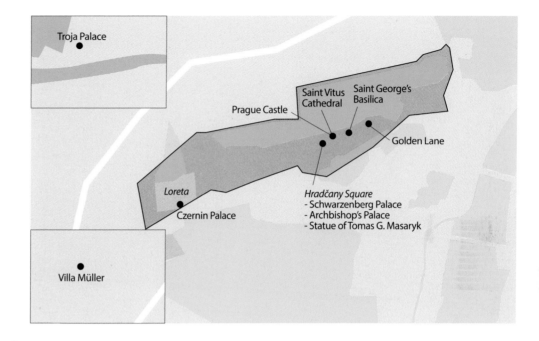

The walls of Prague Castle, interrupted briefly by the steeple of Saint George's Basilica, are a key feature of the Prague skyline. The Prague Castle is not a single building, but an entire neighborhood that has sat on this hill for close to nine centuries, where it has served as the seat of political might, administrative power, and religious authority. Prague Castle is a city within the city—a series of buildings in styles from Romanesque to Art Nouveau. Art, history, objects, and memories of earth-shaking events and impressive figures intertwine here. From the entrance to the Belvedere garden, astonishing images accumulate. Saint Vitus Cathedral houses the Bohemian crown jewels. The cathedral is itself a jewel of the fourteenth-century Gothic and an apt symbol of the glory and tragedy of Prague's history. The triple-aisle choir with ambulatory and radiating chapels dates to the fourteenth century. After Charles IV died in 1378, construction slowed and then ground to a halt. Later rulers focused instead on the reception rooms in the castle itself with spectacular results, such as the late Gothic vaults designed by Benedikt Ried in the late fifteenth century. Attention then shifted once again, this time to the Golden Lane. Work on the cathedral got underway again in 1871, when work on other Gothic cathedrals (such as those in Cologne, Barcelona, and Milan) also restarted and architecture worldwide began to change direction and develop a revival style that was headed toward modernism.

OPPOSITE: PRAGUE CASTLE IN WINTER. PRAGUE COMBINES STRAIGHT LINES (THE CHARLES BRIDGE, THE CASTLE, THE SPIRES OF THE CATHEDRAL) AND SOFTER SHAPES (THE BAROQUE DOMES OF THE CHURCH OF SAINT NICHOLAS IN MALÁ STRANA AT LEFT).

# HRADČANY SQUARE
### Hradčanské náměstí

Hradčany Square, on a gently sloping hill, is surrounded on all sides by large buildings. Opposite the castle is the baroque Tuscany Palace, once home to the Grand Duke of Tuscany, its twin entrances topped by matching towers. To the left is the sixteenth-century Schwarzenberg Palace with lovely sgraffito decorations. Views of the Malá Strana rooftops can be glimpsed between the buildings.

## SCHWARZENBERG PALACE
### *Schwarzenberský palác*

The Renaissance-style Schwarzenberg Palace is located at the upper end of Hradčany, atop the hill that runs down toward Malá Strana. The building's exterior is decorated with sgraffito that gives it the look of rustication. The interior houses the baroque painting and sculpture collection of the Prague National Gallery.

## ARCHBISHOP'S PALACE  ▶
### *Arcibiskupský palác*

The white exterior of the eighteenth-century Archbishop's Palace is another landmark on Hradčany Square, just steps from the gate to the Castle's outer courtyard. The spires of the cathedral can be seen in the background.

## STATUE OF TOMAS G. MASARYK
### *Pomník T. G. Masaryka*

Just inside the Prague Castle area stands the Archbishop's Palace, and in front of it a potent symbol of national independence, the statue of Tomas G. Masaryk. Masaryk was the first president of the Czechoslovak Republic in 1918.

# PRAGUE CASTLE
## *Pražský hrad*

▶

Prague Castle is an enormous complex of buildings constructed over seven centuries. It has a total of about 700 rooms, five churches and chapels, and an endless collection of windows, towers, alleys, and gardens. Indeed, Prague Castle is a living museum of Bohemian history. Perhaps the best way to experience it is to wander through its squares and down its streets and soak up the enchanting atmosphere.

PP. 154-155: A SERIES OF COURTYARDS MARKS PRAGUE CASTLE.
THE FIRST, AN EXTERIOR COURTYARD REACHED BY PASSING THROUGH
A GATE, STANDS IN FRONT OF THE MAIN ENTRANCE. THE SPIRES OF
THE CATHEDRAL SOAR OVERHEAD.
OPPOSITE: THE MATTHIAS GATE BUILT IN THE EARLY 1600S
ECHOES MOTIFS POPULARIZED BY GIULIO ROMANO. LARGE STONE
SCULPTURES ARE LOCATED ALONG THE LENGTH OF THE EIGHTEENTH-
CENTURY FENCE.

PP. 158-159: PRAGUE CASTLE'S THIRD COURTYARD SURROUNDS
SAINT VITUS CATHEDRAL. THIS PHOTO WAS TAKEN FROM THE TOP OF
THE STEEPLE. JOŽE PLECNIK (1928–1932) DESIGNED THE PAVING AND
THE LAYOUT, AS WELL AS AN OBELISK MEMORIALIZING THE FALLEN OF
WORLD WAR I.

ABOVE AND OPPOSITE: ROOMS IN THE ROYAL PALACE HAVE BEEN
DESTROYED BY FIRE SEVERAL TIMES, BUT A FEW OF THE LATE GOTHIC
ROOMS DESIGNED BY BENEDIKT RIED HAVE SURVIVED INTACT.
ELABORATE VAULTS ARE THEIR MOST NOTABLE FEATURE.

LEFT AND RIGHT: THE MOST SIGNIFICANT CHARACTERISTIC SHARED BY THE BUILDINGS MAKING UP PRAGUE CASTLE IS AN ELEGANT AND LINEAR LATE-EIGHTEENTH-CENTURY STYLE THAT SET ASIDE ROCOCO FANTASY FOR EARLY NEOCLASSICISM. ONE WING HOUSES A PAINTING GALLERY EXHIBITING SOME OF THE WORKS COLLECTED BY RUDOLF II. PRAGUE CASTLE IS ALSO KNOWN FOR ITS LUSH GARDENS. THE AREAS ALONG THE WALLS, DESIGNED BY JOŽE PLECNIK, ARE PARTICULARLY LOVELY AND OVERLOOK MALÁ STRANA, THE VLTAVA, AND OLD TOWN. FOLLOWING PAGES: THE ROYAL GARDEN RUNS ALONG THE NORTHERN SIDE OF PRAGUE CASTLE AND INCLUDES THE BELVEDERE PAVILION, A RENAISSANCE JEWEL DESIGNED BY ITALIAN ARCHITECTS IN THE MID-1500S FOR EMPEROR FERDINAND I.

## SAINT VITUS CATHEDRAL
### *Katedrála Sv. Vita*

◀ ▼ ▶▶

Saint Vitus Cathedral is nothing short of a jewel. A prime example of fourteenth-century Gothic architecture in Europe, it is one of Prague's most fascinating buildings.

The Bohemian crown jewels are kept here. The building's impressive qualities are even more astonishing when you consider that it remained half-built for centuries. The chorus area dates to the fourteenth century. This fabulous structure with three aisles, an ambulatory, and radiating chapels with flying buttresses was begun in 1344 by French architect

Matthias of Arras. Swedish architect Peter Parler took over in 1353 and designed the justly famous intricately lined vaults. In about 1370, Venetian artists created a mosaic depicting *Universal Judgment* that decorates the arches of the Golden Gate at the cathedral's main entrance. Work then came to a halt, but was restarted in the latter half of the 1800s. The building was finally completed in 1929, with the earlier and later stages of the project seamlessly combined. While the architectural style remained faithful to its fourteenth-century roots, the decoration of the cathedral evolved over time, so that the building includes Art Nouveau-style windows by Alfons Mucha.

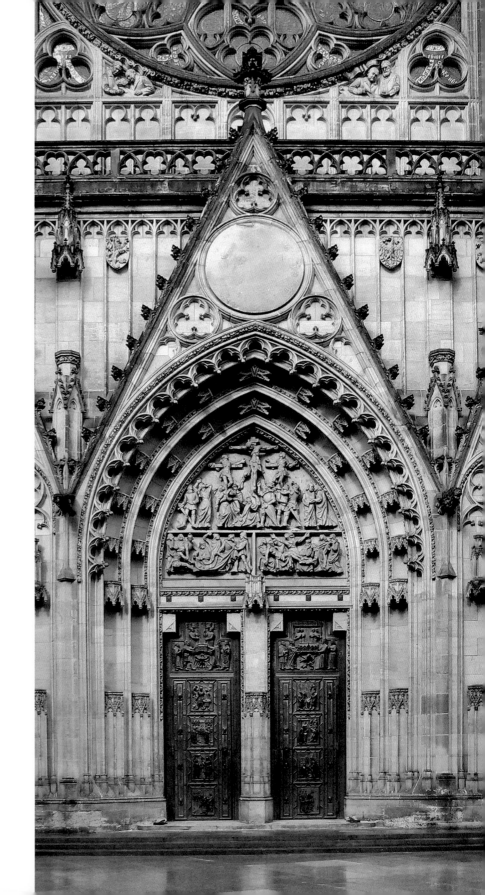

§ᐧ PꝛOCOꝑYUS § ᐧ Fꝛ IꙄ MUꝶ DUꙄ § ᐧ Vꝶ TUꙄ §

# SAINT GEORGE'S BASILICA
### *Bazilika Sv. Jiří*

Saint George's Basilica sits in Saint George's Square, located next to the apse of the cathedral. This building has been modified many times over the years through rebuilding and restoration, but the interior still reflects the twelfth-century Romanesque style. The exterior and the adjacent Chapel of Saint John of Nepomuk are both baroque. The monastery next door houses the National Gallery's nineteenth-century holdings.

# GOLDEN LANE ▶

## *Zlatá ulička*

The Golden Lane is a charming street near the walls of the Prague Castle district. Goldsmiths and other craftspeople who created items for the royal family once lived in the tiny houses that date to the seventeenth and eighteenth centuries. The street has been lovingly restored and is a popular tourist destination.

## HRADČANY NEIGHBORHOOD
*Hradčany - ulice*

The Hradčany neighborhood has more to offer than imposing buildings. It also has tranquil corners and peaceful spots along quiet side streets lined with small historic houses.

# LORETA ▶
## *Loreta* ▶▶

Loreta Square is one of the prettiest in Prague. It's located in the center of the Hradčany neighborhood just outside the Prague Castle district and is home to several large baroque buildings. The Loreta, which has a wonderful eighteenth-century exterior, sits inside a courtyard with porticos. It is a reproduction of the Basilica della Santa Casa in Loreto, Italy, and houses a collection of interesting liturgical and votive items.

## CZERNIN PALACE
### *Černinsky palàc*

The substantial Czernin Palace stretches almost 500 feet (150 meters) across from Loreta. It was built by Italian architects in the seventeenth century and displays some late Renaissance features, including the rusticated base on the ground floor and the large Corinthian demi-columns that run along the upper floors.

## VILLA MÜLLER ▶
### *Müllerova vila*

Various twentieth-century villas can be found a short distance from the Castle in the elegant Střešovice neighborhood in the north of the city. One standout is the home built in 1928 by modern architect Adolf Loos. Stripped of any decoration in order to showcase its clear-cut geometric precision, the villa still has its original furnishings, which were also designed by Loos.